I Will Always Love and Forgive You

Written by Sarah Seiz

Illustrated by Layla Seiz

Published by: Little Light Shine Bright

ISBN: 978-1-7923-9917-6

Subject Heading: CHRISTIAN LIVING/ PARENTING/ CHILDREN/ LOVE/ FORGIVENESS

www.littlelightshinebright.com

Dedications:

SS: Layla and Lilo—there is nothing you could ever do to make me stop loving you. Thank God, EVERYTHING is forgiven through the cross. And to Steven—without your loving push to keep going, this book might still be trapped in my laptop.

LS: In loving memory of my Nana, Lee Ann Thompson—thank you for funding this book and making it happen. Also, to my mom and dad—thank you for being really good parents and demonstrating love and forgiveness.

With Gratitude:

Lisa Albinus, interior/exterior designer extraordinaire and friend.
Thank you for pulling this all together!

Contents

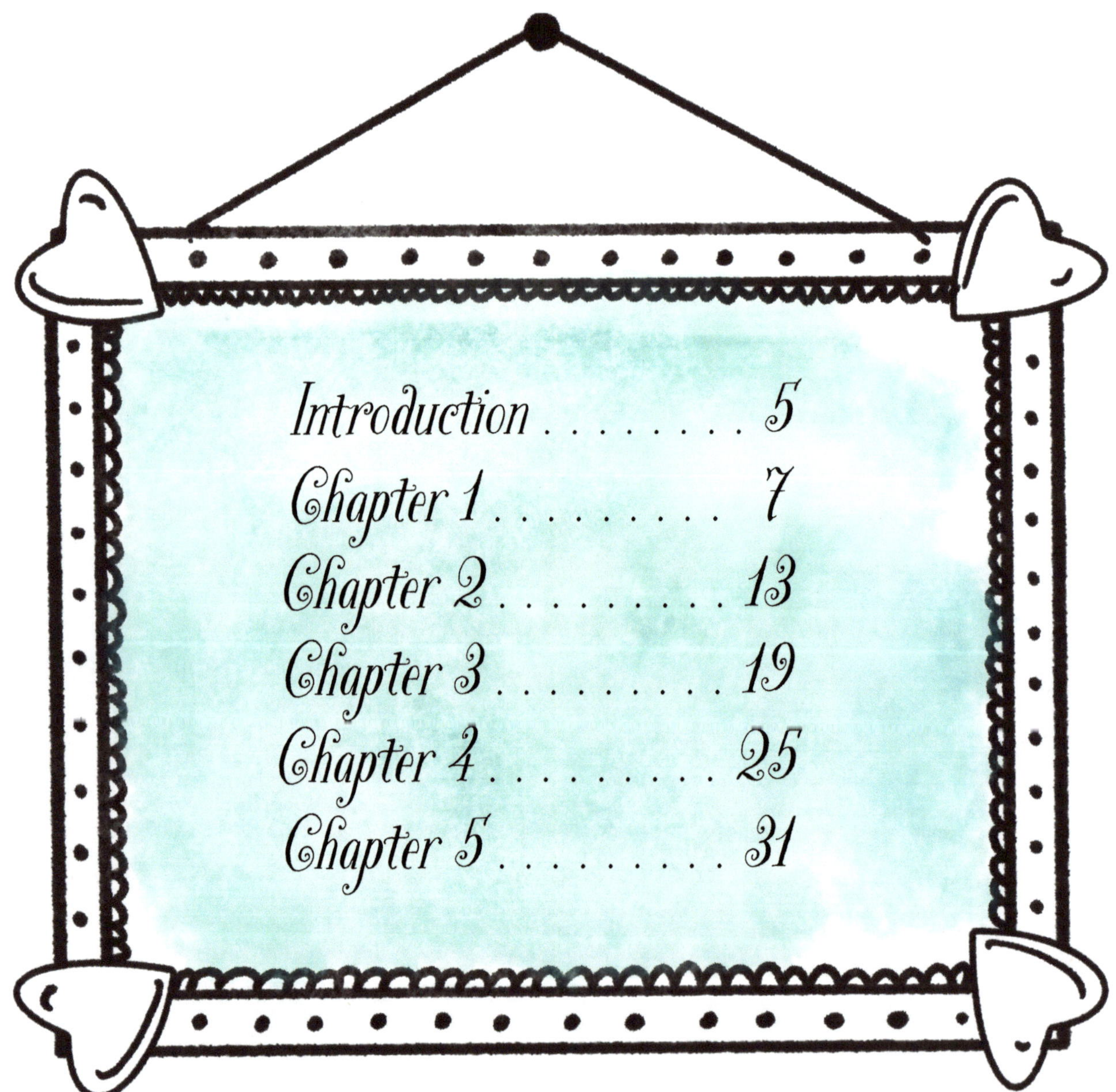

Children are a precious gift,
a heavenly blessing from above.
God made parents earthly guardians,
to give and teach *unconditional love*.

Chapter 1

Jack was an energetic child,
who loved to wrestle and act tough.
One day he hurt Mommy in a tackle,
that was playfully too rough.

She quickly paused the game,
to examine her painful injury.
Her son looked over with tears
and asked, "Do you still love me?"

"Of course, I still love you,"
Mommy said to her son.
Then she pulled Jack closer
to hug and kiss him a ton.

Mommy knew that he needed
to be reminded every single day.
"I will always love and forgive you,"
is what she would repeatedly say.

Chapter 2

13

Kaylee liked to be independent,
and do things all by herself.
One day she reached way up high
on the top refrigerator shelf.

She accidentally dropped and spilled
the milk all over the floor.
Kaylee ran over to her Daddy crying,
"Do you still love me anymore?"

"Of course, I still love you,"
he said to his worried daughter.
Daddy knew this was an unfailing
truth that he had already taught her.

But children need to be reminded
each and every single day.
"I will always love and forgive you,"
is what Daddy continued to say.

17

Chapter 3

One day play time was over and
Jack was asked to put away his toys.
He didn't feel like cleaning up the mess,
so he angrily shouted and made noise.

Jack stomped his feet loudly
and threw a tantrum on the floor.
Then he yelled mean words and said,
"Daddy, I don't like you anymore!"

After he had time to cool down,

Jack came back to apologize.

He turned to his father feeling awful,

with a teary, sad look in his eyes.

Daddy comforted him and said,
"I will always love and forgive you.
This includes the hurtful words you say,
and the regretful things you may do."

Chapter 4

Kaylee loved to eat sugary sweets,
so she snuck a scoop of cookie dough.
When Mommy asked if she had taken some,
She felt scared and answered, "No."

Immediately Kaylee felt guilty,
then she panicked and began to cry.
She felt sad about sneaking,
and then on top of that told a lie.

"I'm sorry I took something without
permission," Kaylee began to say.
"Then I made it worse by lying about it . . .
this feels like the absolute worst day!"

28

Mommy thanked her for telling the truth
and admitting to her wrongdoing.
"I will always love you and forgive you,
for it is your heart that I am pursuing."

Chapter 5

The children thought hard about
the different choices they both make.
Some bad things were done on purpose,
and some were accidentally a mistake.

Either way they soon realized,

the result was always the same.

After each and every wrong doing,

love and forgiveness always came.

33

Kaylee and Jack still didn't understand.
Their curiosity remained.
So they went straight to their parents,
to ask if it could be explained.

"Why do you always love and forgive us,
whenever we act bad?
How do you do this instead of
yelling at us or staying mad?"

The parents turned to their children,
with affection in their eyes.
They tenderly told them the example was
already given by someone very wise.

The reason for these actions could be
found in the Bible and in their heart.
God designed a grand rescue plan
so that sin could never keep us apart.

The power of the cross covered
every single bad choice and mistake.
Jesus lovingly gave the gifts of
mercy and grace for everyone's sake.

Jesus took the punishment for our sins,
then He rose up from the grave.
Now His children can have eternal life,
all because *He first loved and forgave.*

The only reason heaven holds a spot
for believers in God's family,
is because *our Savior already loved and
forgave all* by paying the ultimate fee.

Jesus taught us an incredible example,
and He wants us to pass it along too.
This is how *God's love and forgiveness spreads,*
by the things we choose to say and do.

The parents pulled their children closer,
to check and see if they understood.
Hoping it now made more sense,
after hearing how God is so good!

"That is why no matter what,

we will always love and forgive you.

This is the greatest lesson we were taught

and what all of us are expected to do."

If you are interested in having Sarah as a guest speaker, please visit her website at:

www.littlelightshinebright.com

to learn more.

About the Author

SARAH SEIZ loves to read, write, bake, drink chai tea lattes, and eat cake! She previously published her first book, *Purpose Through Perspective (30 Letters Of Encouragement For 30 Days Of Spiritual Growth.)* Now she is excited to jump into writing children's books, and feels especially blessed to team up with her daughter as the illustrator.

About the Illustrator

LAYLA SEIZ is in her freshman year of high school. Some of her interests include: swimming, art, and baking. She is so excited to be illustrating this book with her Mom!